Animal Survival

ANIMAL
RELATIONSHIPS

Michel Barré

Gareth Stevens Publishing
MILWAUKEE

— The author would like to thank Jack Guichard and Maurice Berteloot for their encouragement, critical opinions, and advice during the progress of this series.

The U.S. editor would like to thank Jan W. Rafert, Curator of Primates and Small Mammals, Milwaukee County Zoo, Milwaukee, Wisconsin, for his kind and professional help with the information in this book.

For a free color catalog describing Gareth Stevens' list of high-quality books and multimedia programs, call 1-800-542-2595 (USA) or 1-800-461-9120 (Canada). Gareth Stevens Publishing's Fax: (414) 225-0377. See our catalog, too, on the World Wide Web: http://gsinc.com

Library of Congress Cataloging-in-Publication Data

Barré, Michel, 1928-
  [Relations entre animaux. English]
  Animal relationships / by Michel Barré.
    p. cm. — (Animal survival)
  Includes bibliographical references (p. 47) and index.
  Summary: Examines how animals relate to one another, discussing predators, parasites, animals that move in groups, and other topics, particularly animal communication.
  ISBN 0-8368-2077-0 (lib. bdg.)
  1. Social behavior in animals—Juvenile literature. 2. Animal communication—Juvenile literature. [1. Animals—Habits and behavior. 2. Animal communication.] I. Title. II. Series: Barré, Michel, 1928- Animal survival.
QL775.B2713 1998
591.56—dc21   97-31859

This North American edition first published in 1998 by
Gareth Stevens Publishing
1555 North RiverCenter Drive, Suite 201
Milwaukee, Wisconsin 53212 USA

Translated from the French by Janet Neis.
U.S. editor: Rita Reitci
Editorial assistant: Diane Laska

Series consultant: Michel Tranier, zoologist at the French National Museum of Natural History.

The editors wish to thank the Jacana Agency and the artists who kindly granted permission to use the photographs displayed in the following pages:

Cover, P. Laboute, Ferrero-Labat, P.H.R. Sefton; 4, P. Pilloud; 5, Ferrero-Labat; 6, F. Ramade; 7, C. Gautier, J.-P. Heruy; 8, H. Chaumeton; 9, Varin-Visage, H. Chaumeton; 10, Ferrero-Labat; 11, Labat-Lanceau; 12, Varin-Visage; 13, Y. Arthus-Bertrand; 14, D. Guravich-PHR, Varin-Visage; 15, Mammifrance; 16, G. Robertson-AUS; 17, M. Danegger; 18, D. Lippmann; 18-19, C. Haagner; 20, J.-M. Labat, Frédéric; 21, A. Degré; 22, M.-C. Noailles, P. Lorne; 23, J.-P. Heruy; 24, 25, Varin-Visage; 26, F. Pölking; 27, Ferrero-Labat, R. Volot; 28, B. Rebouleau, A. Carey-PHR; 29, J.-L. Dubois; 30, A. Gandolfi; 31, J.-F. Hellio, N. Van Ingen; 32, A. Aigouin; 32-33, S. Krasemann; 33, H. Chaumeton; 34, Rouxaine, S. Cordier; 35, J.-P. Ferrero; 36, K. Ross; 37, J.-P. Saussez, C. and M. Moiton; 38, Varin-Visage; 39, P. Prigent; 40, J.-M. Davenne; 41, A. Le Toquin; 42, G. Ziesler; 43, Varin-Visage; 44, J.-P. Thomas; 45, Varin-Visage

Printed in the United States of America

1 2 3 4 5 6 7 8 9 02 01 00 99 98

CONTENTS

PREDATORS AGAINST PREY

Above: **This graceful dragonfly is a predator.**

In nature, the greatest conflict between animals is predation, where one kind of animal hunts another. Animals called predators find and kill other animals, called prey, to get food.

Predators are named after what they eat: the insectivores prey on insects; piscivores prey on fish; and carnivores prey on animal flesh.

Some of the best-known predators are carnivorous mammals, such as wolves, foxes, wild dogs, martens, lions and other large felines, and birds of prey, such as eagles and falcons. Other predators range across the entire spectrum of animal life. Jellyfish, starfish, sea anemones, some mollusks (such as squid and octopuses), spiders, some insects (such as wasps and dragonflies), most species of crustaceans, amphibians, reptiles, and fish are all predators because they eat other animals.

Vegetarian animals

Many mollusks and insects, most tortoises and rodents, and all hoofed mammals (such as sheep and horses) eat only plants. These animals are called herbivores. They are never predators, but they are often the prey of predators.

Avoiding relatives

Animals usually do not eat other animals of their own species, but they often will eat similar animals. The main exception occurs when a female spider or praying mantis devours the male right after mating with it. The female eats the male in order to provide food for her eggs.

Natural balance

Herbivorous animals in large numbers can do a tremendous amount of damage to a plant community. If they eat plants unchecked, herbivores can quickly and completely destroy a valuable food source.

By eating some of the herbivores, especially the old and the sick, predators help maintain a natural balance and can prevent vegetation from being wiped out.

Eaters eaten

Any predator can be eaten in turn by another predator. This also helps nature stay in balance. The ladybug, a predator of vegetarian aphids, for example, can become the prey of birds.

These birds, in turn, might become the prey of a cat, a bird of prey, or some other predator.

Below: **This lynx — a large, carnivorous, feline predator — has just killed a deer.**

PARASITIC ANIMALS

Animals that live on and feed off of other animals without killing them are called parasites. The animals they live and feed on are called hosts.

Some parasites, such as the bedbug, the female mosquito, and the leech, lead a relatively independent life. They suck the blood of other animals. Some parasites, such as the louse, the flea, and some mites, move very little. They live for long periods of time on the animal from which they obtain food, although they can move from one host to another. These are called ectoparasites because they live on the outside of their hosts.

Some parasites do not move around. Instead, they attach themselves to any host that comes near them. This is how the larvae of mites travel. They grow under the skin of humans or animals that touch the plants where the larvae are waiting. Some small mollusks live encrusted in the flesh of a starfish or a sea urchin.

Many parasites are worms of various kinds.

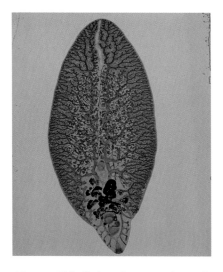

Above: **This fluke, shown enlarged under a microscope, attacks the cells of its host's liver.**

As animals swallow these worms, most often as eggs, they develop inside an organ in the host's body. Trichina worms, for example, are parasites that, if swallowed in the larva stage, will quickly mature, reproduce, and infect the host with an intestinal disease called trichinosis. Other intestinal parasites include pinworms, round worms, and tapeworms. Parasites that live inside their hosts are called endoparasites.

Developing by stages

Parasites can travel through more than one host as they develop. For instance, a parasitic worm can be swallowed first by a crustacean, which then is eaten by a fish. This fish can then be eaten by a fish-eating bird.

The fluke parasite's egg develops first inside a water snail. When it becomes a larva, it leaves the snail and attaches itself to a plant near water. At this stage, a mammal that comes to graze can easily swallow it. Once inside, the fluke attaches itself to the liver of its permanent host.

Disease spreaders

Parasites can cause pain, itching, and infections. The ascarids, or round worms, are responsible for some allergies and asthma. These illnesses often will weaken the host but usually do not kill it. However, parasites can carry microbes and pass these on to the host. These bacteria and one-celled animals sometimes cause illness or death.

For example, some mosquitoes carry terrible diseases, such as malaria and yellow fever.

Several centuries ago, fleas became infected with, carried, and transferred the bacteria that caused epidemics of the plague, or Black Death, throughout the world.

Tse-tse flies carry and transmit the parasites that cause sleeping sickness. Body lice sometimes carry typhoid.

Parasitic young

Some species of birds, such as the cuckoo, lay their eggs in the nests of other birds. The cuckoo abandons its eggs and leaves the care of its young to the other birds.

One species of wasp paralyzes caterpillars or other insects then lays eggs on them. When the eggs hatch, the young devour their hosts.

Below: The flea, carried by rats, has spread the microbes of the Black Death.

Bottom: The tse-tse fly's abdomen swells with the blood it drank. If the fly has picked up sleeping sickness, it can transmit it to the humans it bites.

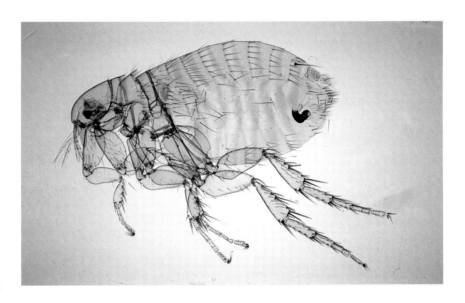

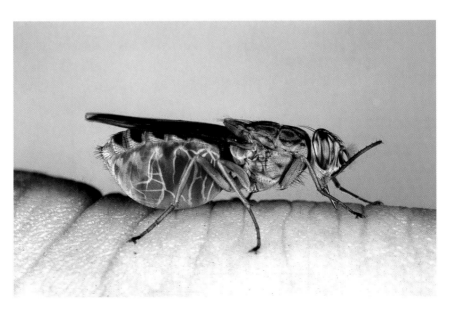

ASSOCIATIONS BETWEEN DIFFERENT SPECIES

Above: **The hermit crab, a crustacean with a soft belly, lives protected in the abandoned shell of another animal. A sea anemone also may attach itself to the shell.**

Different animal species sometimes have relationships that seem strange or unusual to humans.

Getting shelter

Many tiny invertebrates live in the cavities of sponges, where they find protection. Small crabs often hide inside the shell of a mussel. These tiny animals do not do any harm — they only seek shelter. The burrowing shrimp digs a hole in the sand where a fish might come to live with it.

In warm seas, the clown fish lives freely among the deadly tentacles of a sea anemone. This fish carries the anemone's own scent.

The clown fish eats the debris left from the sea anemone's meals. The poisonous tentacles of the anemone, which paralyze other species of fish, will also protect the clown fish from its own group of unwelcome predators.

Another unusual partnership exists between the hermit crab and the sea anemone. The hermit crab carries the anemone around on its shell, and when the crab outgrows its shell and begins the search for a new one, the anemone moves right along with it. The sea anemone gets a home and the leftovers of the crustacean's meals.

The hermit crab, in return, is protected from its natural enemies by the sea anemone's stinging, poisonous tentacles.

Helping out

In grasslands, some types of birds commonly

Left: **These birds clean up the insect larvae that live on the skin of this buffalo.**

perch on top of buffaloes, antelopes, giraffes, and rhinoceroses. The birds do not intend harm to these large mammals. Instead, they eat the parasitic larvae on their skin. Each animal gains from this odd relationship. The birds get food, and their quick, noisy reactions to the slightest hints of danger warn the larger animals.

Some fish species, such as the wrasse, also eat parasites. In doing this, the wrasse clean the scales and gills of fish that are much larger than they are. The larger fish do not attack the cleaners, even though they could easily swallow these smaller fish.

Sharks allow a type of fish called remora to attach themselves to the shark's skin and clean it. The sharks provide free transportation to the fish in return.

The badger and the honey-guide bird, a type of cuckoo in tropical

Below: **The wrasse cleans other fish.**

countries, also have an unusual relationship. The bird points out and leads the badger to a beehive. Immune to bee stings, the badger pulls down the hive and eats the honey. The bird, which also likes honey, gets the leftovers.

When red ants find a caterpillar that secretes a sweet liquid, they carry it back to their warm underground anthill for the winter. The ants lick the sweet liquid, and the caterpillar eats a few ant larvae. In spring, the caterpillar transforms into a butterfly and leaves the anthill to find a mate and lay eggs.

EATING SIDE BY SIDE

The ability to eat a meal in the same place is the most common relationship between animal neighbors.

Being together

Animals from the same species often eat together, but not because they gather there intentionally. For instance, many aphids will lick sap from the same plant because they were born from the same mother. This behavior is also true of caterpillars hatched from the same cluster of eggs laid by a female butterfly.

Also, as soon as certain plants bloom, bees come together from many hives to gather nectar.

Sharing space

On the African savanna, different herbivores, such as antelopes, zebras, and giraffes, often live in the same place. They are not rivals because they do not eat the same plants or the same parts of these plants. Some prefer the tender shoots; others choose the stems or the large leaves.

Neighboring animals also will go to the same water hole when they want to drink or bathe.

Above: **Zebras and gnus graze side by side on this savanna in Kenya.**

Above: **Hatched from the same butterfly's eggs, these caterpillars eat the leaves of the same oak tree.**

11

Hunting or Fishing Together

Above: **Flying in a group, these cormorants drive fish into shallow water, making it easier for each bird to catch a meal.**

Large groups of prey that travel together will sometimes attract a large number of predators that ordinarily do not travel together. Grizzly bears, for instance, gather during the annual migration of salmon when these fish travel upriver to mate and lay eggs. This is a good opportunity for bears to catch fish.

At low tide, water birds dig in the sand for worms and crustaceans. Each of the birds hunts for different prey that lives as deep in the sand as the bird's beak is long. There is no competition or fighting for food among these bird species.

Hunting together

Groups of cormorants or pelicans sometimes gather in a semicircle and flap their wings to scare fish and make them move toward shallow water, where they are much easier to catch.

Wolves, jackals, hyenas, and lions hunt in groups. Their usual technique

Above: **Hyenas hunt in groups. When they kill, vultures quickly gather to grab some of the food.**

is to approach a herd of hoofed herbivores, such as antelopes, zebras, giraffes, and gnus, and look for the sick or weaker animals. When the predators attack, they work together to cut one of the animals out of the herd, circle it, and kill it.

13

Moving in
a Crowd

Above: **Millions of monarch butterflies migrate from Canada to Mexico, where they reproduce.**

Some insects, such as midges and mosquitoes, often move in swarms. Reacting to the same heat and humidity, they gather in groups just by chance. Also, at night, several types of insects can be drawn together by a light.

During mating season, eels leave their rivers and swamps to mate and lay eggs in the Sargasso Sea, in the Atlantic Ocean. Larvae hatch and travel back to their parents' home. Salmon and some crab species also travel in groups to reproduce.

During migration, some animals just find them-selves together at the same time. Some of the migrating animals will also react to the calls of others of their species. For instance, migrating locusts send out a certain sound as they travel that signals a need to search for food. In a similar way, in autumn, migrat-ing birds will gather and call to each other.

Monarch butterflies travel in large groups from Canada to Mexico to spend the winter.

Some birds, such as cranes and geese, fly in a formation, usually a *V*, and take turns flying in front against the full force of the wind.

Many fish species travel in schools. They find their way through the scent and sight of their neighbors' scales.

Some animals that live in independent families will gather temporarily into a larger herd to search for food. Reindeer and elephants do this.

Every few years, small European rodents called lemmings increase in great numbers. When they have used up all the food supply in their area, they begin a massive migration. This instinct is so strong that they try to cross rivers or the sea, even though they drown. Many lemmings are eaten by fish, birds, and other predators these huge migrations attract.

Below: **Each autumn, swallows make the long migration to a warmer climate.**

GATHERING TO SLEEP OR HIBERNATE

Above: **Bats sleep and hibernate in colonies.**

Geckos hunt alone at night, but they prefer to sleep in small groups. Some birds, such as the starlings, usually spend their nights in groups in a tree. Bats usually sleep in large colonies in a cave or other dark cavity.

When the cold winter arrives, marmots change burrows and hibernate together. Bats also gather and hibernate in colonies.

Carp and some species of salamanders spend the cold weather together at the bottom of the swamp.

LIFE AS A
COUPLE

Many animals, when not mating, live alone. In many species, the young animals do not live with their mothers and fathers. In fact, many of these young animals never even know their parents, which often go their separate ways right after mating.

Birds usually will live in couples, not only to take turns protecting the eggs, but also to help with the burden of feeding the baby birds.

When the young birds are ready to leave the nest and live on their own, their parents will often remain together to raise a new brood.

Some bird couples stay together until the next migration, as swallows do. Other bird couples do not separate for several more years.

Some species, such as ravens and some parrot species are very faithful and never leave their mate. Swans and storks also remain as couples for their entire lives, in spite of migrations.

Groups of couples

Some birds, such as crows, like to group their nests together. Other types of birds, such as the sociable weavers, build their nests under the same roof structure.

Many birds live in dense colonies among rocks, as auks do, or on sea ice, as with Emperor penguins.

Each bird couple has its own particular place among the huge crowd of nests and usually remains independent of the others in the colony.

Left: **A colony of emperor penguins in Antarctica. The young are grouped together so the adults can protect them from predators.**

Above: **A pair of storks with their young.**

ONE MALE, SEVERAL FEMALES, AND BABIES

Mammal mothers nurse and care for their babies. In some species, a family group includes several females with their babies and just one male.

In deer families, a male will dominate a herd of females. He will chase away other males that come near his group.

The same kind of close, nurturing behavior often is found among wild hippopotamuses, horses, zebras, and sea elephants.

Female groups

Female elephants will organize groups, mostly of relatives, to protect and care for their young. An experienced female leads the others. The females do not allow males in their group. Only in mating season do they associate with males.

Left: **Each male sea elephant protects his group of females from other males.**

Above: **Female elephants live in family groups and keep males away.**

LARGE FAMILIES

Above: **A pack of wolves howls to signal possession of hunting territory to their rivals.**

Below: **Cleaning each other's hair is a sign of affection among baboons.**

Some mammal species live in large groups of ten or more individuals. These animals include wolves, lions, hyenas, and monkeys.

Within each group, the animals usually establish a system of dominance. One animal becomes the leader until it becomes too old, at which time a younger, stronger animal takes over as leader.

With wolves, it is a male and female pair that dominates. These two often prevent others in the pack from having young. All the young of a wolf pack are from the lead pair.

In troops of monkeys, the males have several levels of dominance, from the very lowest, which is dominated by all the rest, to the top monkey, which dominates all the others. The dominant female's young have the best chance of belonging to upper levels. The others are trained to accept this dominance from birth.

An equal society

The wild dogs of Africa have a communal life without domination. Some adults take care of the young while others hunt. When they return, the hunters regurgitate the food they swallowed, and the entire community eats it together.

Females hunting

Lionesses hunt together. But unlike the female elephants that reject the males, the lionesses allow the lions to take the first and best part of the prey they have killed. They follow this ritual even though the lions do not participate in the hunt.

Above: **Wild dogs attack a zebra. They will take much of the kill back to their pack.**

ANIMALS THAT LIVE ONLY IN GROUPS

Social insects, such as bees, termites, and ants, live together in large numbers. They will not survive if they are isolated permanently from their community in the hive, the termite mound, or the anthill.

Scientists have discovered that each of these insects needs the others to obtain food. Their behavior is guided by the substances and scents they exchange with the members of their large communities.

Nearly all the members of these insect colonies are workers that cannot reproduce. Instead, they take care of the queen's eggs and larvae, gather supplies, and build and maintain the nest.

The only insect that can produce young is the colony's queen. Her job is to reproduce and to enlarge the community by laying eggs constantly.

Above: **Bees have built this hive in a tree.**

Below: **A group of ants can attack an insect much larger than they are.**

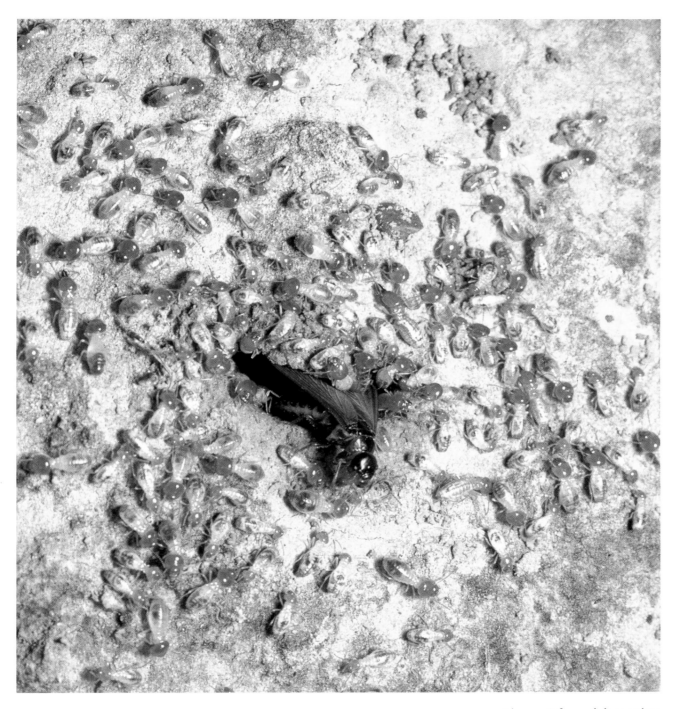

Above: **A few adult termites can start a new family and build another termite mound.**

Conflicts Within the Same Species

Above: **Usually calm, the male buffalo shows its aggression by throwing dirt at its rival. If the rival doesn't leave, the two may fight head to head.**

In some species of mammals, a male that has a relationship with one or a group of females will drive away any rival males. Sometimes this results in duels between males, but they are usually not fatal.

Buffalo, bison, and deer butt heads and push each other around with their antlers. Male giraffes move their necks and beat the other male's chest with their horns. As soon as the rival senses that it is losing, it begins to act in a submissive manner, which stops the fight. The dominant male has proven its strength and allows the loser to leave.

For animals living in groups, such as wolves and monkeys, the male that is dominant often displays its power over other males. The others will adopt a posture of submission. For the wolf, this is a lowered head.

Similar conflicts can also happen among domestic animals, such as cows. The strongest animal challenges the others, forehead to forehead, to show herself as "queen" of the herd.

Marking territory

Animals frequently will mark the limits of the territory that they regard as their private domain, which is forbidden to others of their species. When the area is family

territory, other males are not allowed to remain.

The hunting territory of predators is fairly large. This hunting area could be about 42 square yards (35 square meters) for the lizard, 480 square yards (400 sq. m) for the heron, up to 1 square mile (2.6 sq. kilometers) for the buzzard, and 12 square miles (30 sq. km) for a pride of lions.

Birds announce their home territory by singing. Their cries also can mark hunting territory.

Mammals often mark their ground with urine or droppings. The daily behavior of a male dog might be to sniff nearly everywhere it walks. It may lift a leg to urinate in several places. At the same time dogs deposit urine, they spray a few drops from their scent glands, the way their ancestors did, to mark their territory. A male hippopotamus also marks its territory — with droppings that it spreads out and tramples.

Cats have scent glands on several parts of their body, such as the forehead, cheeks, and tail. Domestic cats mark their territory by rubbing these parts against furniture or people in the house.

In the wild, deer mark territory by rubbing the tear glands of their eyes against branches and trees in their part of the forest.

Above: **This deer is marking its territory by rubbing its tear glands against trees.**

BODY ARMOR OF ANIMALS

Many animals can use certain parts of their body for attack or defense.

Jaws and beaks

The most common defensive or offensive action of one animal against another is biting. Biting, especially by animals with strong jaws and sharp teeth, can make a serious wound. The front teeth, or incisors, of herbivores can cut badly.

Below: **This hippopotamus, too large for the crocodile to attack, is safe from its powerful jaws.**

The canines, or fangs, of a carnivore can kill. The powerful jaws of sharks and crocodiles hold many sharp teeth.

Birds often strike with their beaks to defend themselves or to catch prey. The strong, hooked beak of a bird of prey is a very dangerous weapon.

Insect jaws can also serve as biting weapons. Wasps, grasshoppers, dragonflies, and praying mantises use this method.

Many fish have strong, beaklike mouths to grab their prey.

Grabbing and hitting

Grabbing hold of the other animal is another common animal action. Some animals grab with their tentacles or arms, as do the sea anemone, the octopus, and the starfish. Some crustacean species, including crabs and lobsters, use strong pincers. Scorpions and some insects also have pincers.

The sharp claws of felines, such as lions, tigers, and even domestic cats, make dangerous weapons. Felines attack with their front feet. They retract their claws when walking, so they don't wear down.

Birds of prey have powerful feet and hard claws to grasp prey.

Horses, donkeys, and zebras all use their hooves as weapons by kicking with front and hind feet.

Elephants grab enemies with their trunks and trample with their feet.

Horns and tusks

Many plant-eating, or herbivorous, animals have horns that they use to defend themselves.

Horns are made of a thick material — similar to hooves — that cover two protruding bones on the forehead. Oxen, male goats, and rams have these horns.

Animals related to deer, such as reindeer and moose, have hornlike growths on their head, called antlers. These fall off each year and grow back even larger and with more branches.

Rhinoceroses have a stiff, fibrous horn in the middle of the snout. Some rhinos have two horns, located one in back of the other.

Other animals can use special teeth, called tusks, for defense. These animals can strike or stab enemies with these long teeth. Elephants and wild boars have tusks. The male narwhal, a polar sea mammal, has a single, long, spiral tusk that it uses to fight with other males of its species.

Above: **When they disagree, baboons often bite.**

Below: **The moose has the largest antlers in the deer family.**

27

CHEMICAL AND ELECTRIC DEFENSES

Above: **The stinger at the end of a scorpion's tail can inject a dangerous poison.**

Below: **When the skunk lifts its tail and sprays its irritating scent, its enemies run away.**

Venom

Some animals secrete a liquid poison, called venom. This fluid can paralyze the muscles of an animal's enemies. Cobra venom can stop the heart from beating. Rattlesnake and viper venom can cause internal bleeding. The venom of scorpions can do all of the above at the same time.

The venom of spiders and some insects, such as wasps and bees, is not as poisonous, but is still dangerous. However, the venom of some spiders can harm humans.

Snakes and spiders inject their poison into victims with hollow fangs in their mouth. Scorpions, bees, wasps, and hornets use a stinger at the end of their tail or abdomen.

The tentacles of jellyfish and sea anemones contain poisonous stinging cells. But the sea slug can eat jellyfish and sea anemones without risk and add the stinging cells to its own body. This protects the sea slug from predators.

Some animals, such as cobras and certain ants, spray venom at the enemy to blind it.

A toad's skin is covered with venom glands. This provides toads with some protection. Predators will spit the skin out and never attack toads again.

A foul defense

A polecat's anal gland can spray a foul liquid to confuse a tracking dog's sense of smell. A skunk's spray scent is even worse. It can confuse tracking animals for a long time.

Electric shock
Torpedoes (electric rays) and electric eels have organs made of small electric plates that can send out electric shocks. These shocks, which can be very powerful, will temporarily paralyze or stun prey and enemies.

Above: **This flat fish, a torpedo ray, sends out paralyzing electric shocks.**

ANIMALS CAN PROTECT THEMSELVES

Above: **These young hedgehogs already have quills for protection.**

Body protection

Some animals' bodies are protected by a shell, such as mollusks; by a hard outer cover, such as pangolins, crustaceans, armadillos, and turtles; or by prickly quills, such as sea urchins, hedgehogs, and porcupines.

No protection is ever complete, however, and many of these animals still become the prey of hungry predators.

Fleeing danger

One common defense against a predator or an enemy is to run and look quickly for a safe place to hide. To be able to flee in time, an animal must be aware of the approaching danger.

Species that live in groups usually have one animal looking out for danger. Marmots watch in this way.

Most animals establish an approach or warning zone. Strangers that enter this zone will cause them to run or hide, sometimes after sounding a warning alarm for other animals.

Playing tricks

Some birds that live on the ground, such as larks, know their young will be unprotected if they flee. These birds will pretend to be hurt and move around with difficulty, as if a wing or a foot is wounded or broken. The predator follows, thinking it will be easy to catch this wounded bird. When it has lured the predator far enough away from its nest, the bird quickly flies away, much to the predator's surprise.

Staying still

Some animals, not built for fleeing, remain still, blending in with their surroundings.

Swamp birds, such as the bittern, point their beaks upward in case of danger, staying as still as the clumps of reeds that surround them. Some insects, such as walking sticks, play dead when they feel threatened.

Below: **This bittern points its beak straight up to show the stripes that help it hide among the tall reeds.**

THE ADVANTAGES OF BEING HARD TO SEE

In water, most fish have a light-colored belly that cannot be seen easily by a predator from below; a predator coming from above would not see the fish's dark back, which blends in perfectly with the water bottom.

Left: **The leopard's spots make it difficult to see.**

Many animals are nearly invisible in their natural environment. Prey need to remain unnoticed or they will fall victim to predators. Predators, in turn, must be able to approach prey unseen, or they will miss an opportunity for food.

Camouflage

In nature, a spotted form attracts less attention than a solid one. Many animal species have a spotted body, such as leopards, pythons, and frogs; or a striped body, such as tigers and zebras. In some species, only the young have patterns, since they are more likely to be eaten by predators. For instance, young wild boars are striped, and young fawns have spots.

In snowy regions, polar bears need to be white to hunt successfully.

Some animals vary their camouflage by climate. A mountain hare has white fur in winter, and a desert-living hare survives by being tan in color.

Left: **When frightened, the cuttlefish squirts a cloud of ink that hides its escape from a predator.**

Below: **Look closely to see if one of these leaves is actually an insect.**

Mimicking nature

Many insects look like other natural objects. For example, the walking stick resembles a twig. Leaf insects can look like leaves. Some mantids resemble a flower. Many caterpillars can look like a different, inedible animal.

Some moths will have shapes on their wings that, from a distance, look like the eyes of a bird of prey. Predators will stay away.

Camouflage is not an intentional protection. Animals cannot choose to resemble something else. The ones that by chance have mimicry usually live long enough to pass this on to their young. Others without mimicry very often are eaten by predators before they can reproduce.

Inky cloud

The octopus, the squid, and the cuttlefish, when threatened, will shoot out a cloud of ink. This blinds their predators for a while and hides their escape.

33

VISUAL SIGNALS AND MESSAGES

Above: **At night, the female glowworm attracts males with her light.**

Flashy signals

The abdomen of the glowworm, a wingless female firefly, shines at night to attract males.

The females of other kinds of fireflies also flash signals to guide males to them at night. Some predators can imitate this flashing to attract and eat the fireflies. Some deep-water fish have shiny organs that attract prey.

Shiny signs

Shiny scales help fish in schools keep track of their neighbors. In some troops of monkeys, the pink buttocks of the dominant male is used to signal the entire group.

In antelopes, a white badge, called a mirror, on the females serves as a signal to males from far away.

Many species of birds have plumage that differs in color for the males and females.

Mating signals

During mating season, the males in some species of fish and lizards change colors. Some birds have changed the color of their tail feathers to attract females. The peacock is the best-known example. This bird will spread out its back and tail feathers in a spectacular fan.

Many animals perform a special activity or ritual

Above: **These wolves from the same pack show dominance or submission through their actions.**

before mating. This may include a series of poses and movements. Each animal species has its own particular behavior rituals during courtship.

Expressions

In many instances, the actions of an animal will clearly show its intentions. A cat swishes its tail and a dog wags its tail to show joy. A cat raises its fur and lowers its ears to show anger. A dog usually shows anger by growling and baring its teeth. Most animals can express themselves in some way.

Some types of lizards spread their neck flaps to scare enemies away. The porcupine fish puffs up its entire body when it feels threatened.

Above: **By spreading its neck flaps, this lizard suddenly appears larger to enemies.**

35

INSECTS COMMUNICATE BY SOUND

Above: **The male grasshopper rubs its leg over the edge of its wing covers to make sounds.**

Usually, the males of a species send out their calls to the females. Insects produce sound messages in different ways.

For example, the cricket rubs its elytra together.

Elytra are horny shields that protect the crickets' flying wings when they are at rest. The grasshopper rubs its leg over the edge of its tegmen, or wing covers. The locust makes sounds by rubbing the rough thighs of its back legs together.

The cicada will vibrate membranes in the cavities of its abdomen to make the loudest insect sound.

Some insects, such as bees, produce a buzzing with their wings. When a swarm of bees prepares to leave a crowded hive in search of another place to live, their buzzing can be very loud.

The mosquito's whine and the fly's drone are distinctive sounds made by their wings.

The death-watch beetle makes sounds by striking its body against the wood as it gnaws in its burrow.

The sphinx moth makes a squeaking sound by quickly exhaling air out of its body.

Above: **The cicada makes a shrill sound by vibrating membranes.**

Left: **The locust makes sounds by rubbing its legs together.**

Sound Messages of Fish and Amphibians

Above: **The orca is a sea mammal. It calls under water as whales do.**

Noisy fish

For a long time, humans thought the sea was a world of silence. Now we know that's not true. During times of world conflict, scientists with special machines could hear the sounds of submarines and ships. These amazing machines also detected sounds when no vessels were sighted.

Mines set up to explode when triggered by the sound of an approaching ship sometimes exploded seemingly by themselves. Researchers eventually discovered that fish and sea mammals could also make sounds.

Some fish growl, grind their teeth, noisily spread their fins, or pop their bones. Their gills also can produce sounds.

Mussels make sounds by opening and shutting their shells. Lobsters can noisily rub their antennae against their shells.

Sea mammals are no more silent than fish. Whales, for example, make a variety of sounds. Recordings of these "songs" have become popular the world over.

Today, people who fish can use sonar, a kind of radar for ultrasounds, to hear schools of fish. This helps them put their nets in the right places.

Croaking frogs

Male amphibians, such as frogs and toads, call out to the females by inflating their cheeks and the skin of their throats. This action amplifies their croaking. The calls that emerge are different in each species. Sound messages can range from high, flutelike sounds to loud growls.

Above: **The toad inflates the skin of its throat to amplify its croaking.**

BIRD SONGS

Above: **The call of the finch is melodious and varied.**

Songs and calls

Besides singing their melodious songs, birds have calls that are cries.

These cries can be the calls of hungry babies, parents calling to their young, and cries of alarm, sorrow, or farewell.

Different species of birds have their own unique calls. The raven uses up to eight different calls, the woodpecker as many as seventeen.

Species that live hidden in bushes or trees usually will have louder calls.

Their songs

In some species, the male birds call to the female birds in order to attract them and also to warn other males to keep away from their territory.

Some birds repeat the same song over and over. Other birds, such as the thrush, the blackbird, and the nightingale, can make up variations of their songs. The finch and the wren change the melody but keep the same rhythm.

Researchers now have learned that birds born in isolation and brought up without contact with other adults of their species still can sing, but without variation.

Some birds, such as the starling, the jay, and the mockingbird, can imitate the songs of other species. The mynah bird and the parrot can even imitate the human voice.

Regional accents

Researchers have found that birds in migration can recognize the songs of birds from their own region, which helps them stay together. The birds look the same.

However, by recording and listening carefully to their cries, scientists have discovered there are slight differences corresponding to accents that occur in human languages. This is similar to people of the United States being able to distinguish a New Yorker from a Texan just by their accents.

Caller identity

The cries made by her young are recognized by a mother bird. A gull can find its young among hundreds of nests because she recognizes their cries.

A turkey that hears a recording of a turkey call playing in a stuffed toy animal will use its wings to protectively cover the stuffed toy. However, the same bird will take no interest if it comes across a young turkey covered by a glass jar. A deaf turkey will sometimes kill any young turkeys it comes across because it cannot recognize them as fellow turkeys.

Other sounds

Songs and cries are not the only way birds send messages by sound. The mute swan, which is voiceless, claps its beak noisily. Stork couples greet each other in a similar way. Woodpeckers send messages by quickly tapping on tree trunks. At times, beating wings and swishing tails can serve as warning signals or signs of departure.

Below: **Though their cries seem alike, gulls recognize each other by hearing differences.**

MAMMAL CALLS

Above: **In case of danger, the marmot keeping watch whistles to warn the others.**

Most mammals make sounds characteristic of their species. Only the giraffe makes sounds so rarely that it seems to have no voice.

The wide range of sound messages sent out by mammals varies from the shrill cries of rodents to the loud trumpeting calls of elephants.

As with bird calls, the sounds that mammals make can send different messages, according to the circumstances.

In dogs, most humans can recognize whining and crying, barks of warning, growls of anger, and anguished howling.

Most humans also can distinguish a cat's sounds, whether it meows for food, purrs in pleasure, or hisses in anger.

Deer call only in mating season. The buck calls to attract females and to keep other males away from its territory.

Chamois signal danger to the herd by a hissing

Above: **The gorilla intimidates enemies by beating its chest.**

sound characteristic of these animals. Marmots signal a warning with a repeated, shrill whistle.

Drumming

To warn enemies away, the gorilla beats on its chest like a drum. It may also strike the ground with a tree branch.

By thumping on the ground with its hind feet, a rabbit can quickly warn other rabbits of danger.

Special sounds

Whales "sing" messages to each other. They can navigate by sending out clicking sounds and receiving the echoes.

Dolphins make whistles, which humans can hear, and ultrasounds, which only machines can detect.

Many bats send out shrill, ultrasonic cries as they fly, then listen for the echoes to bounce off obstacles and prey.

DO ANIMALS USE LANGUAGE?

Above: **A worker bee's dance tells its companions where to find a field of flowers.**

The different cries or sounds made by various animals do not really make up a true language.

Scientists are studying whether or not animals can have language that expresses thoughts.

Dancing messenger

When a scout bee finds a large number of flowers, it goes back to the hive to tell its companions. Even if the scout bee is kept from returning to the flowers, the other bees leave the hive and fly in the right direction. An Austrian zoologist, Karl von Frisch, discovered how the bees communicate their message.

When the scout bee returns to the hive, it waves its abdomen and dances in the shape of a figure eight. The axis of the 8 shows the direction. The scent that the scout picked up identifies the kind of flower it found.

Right: **What the dance of the bee in the hive shows.**

Dance in the hive

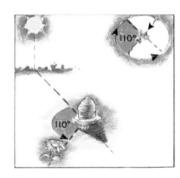

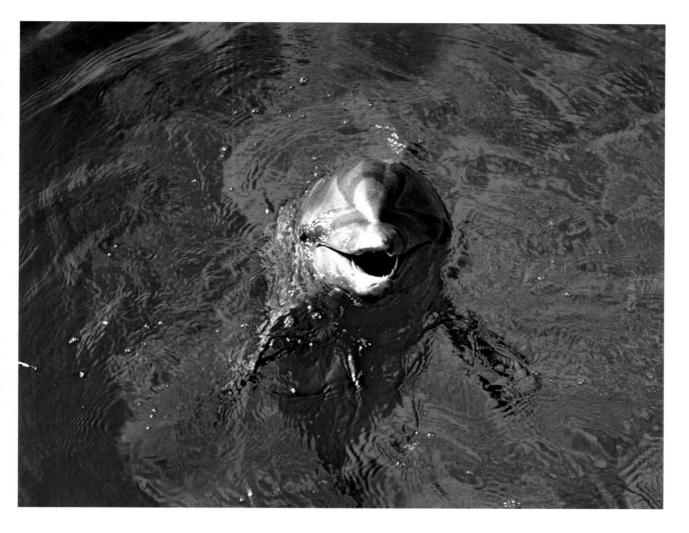

Sign language

Monkeys are unable to pronounce the complex sounds used in human languages. Some scientists, however, believe they can teach monkeys a language of signs and gestures. Monkeys trained in this manner have learned to respond in sign language, which shows advanced intelligence.

Dolphins "speak"

The intelligent dolphins enjoy making contact with humans.

Some people believe the dolphins have a language that is complex enough for humans to exchange detailed messages with these animals.

Researchers still are working to discover if this type of language exists.

Above: **The dolphin likes to communicate, but humans haven't yet discovered a true language to use.**

GLOSSARY

amphibians — cold-blooded vertebrates that have gill-breathing young and air-breathing adults. Frogs and toads are amphibians.

antennae — thin, jointed feelers on the heads of insects and crustaceans.

brood (n) — an animal's young hatched or cared for at the same time.

camouflage — the shape or color pattern an animal has that helps it blend into its surroundings, making it harder for other animals to see.

cavity — space within a mass or an animal's body.

crustaceans — animals with a hard, jointed outer shell that live mostly in water. Crabs and lobsters are crustaceans.

devour — to eat greedily.

environment — the surroundings in which plants and animals live.

fibrous — made up from or having fibers.

herbivores — animals that eat only plants.

hibernate — to enter a state of rest or inactivity in which most bodily functions, such as heartbeat and breathing, slow down. Many animals hibernate during winter.

immune — not affected by.

instinct — a particular behavior pattern that is inborn, not learned.

intimidate — to frighten, or make timid or fearful.

invertebrates — animals that do not have backbones.

isolate — to set or keep apart from others.

larva (_pl_ larvae) — the wingless, wormlike form of a newly-hatched insect; the stage coming after the egg but before full development.

mammals — warm-blooded animals with backbones and hair that bear live young and feed them milk.

mate (v) — to join together (animals) to produce young.

membrane — a thin, flexible tissue layer or covering in a plant or animal that lines or protects a part of its body.

migration — the movement from one place or climate to another, often seasonally.

mimicry — the shape, color, or markings of an animal that resembles another animal or natural object.

mollusks — animals with a hard outer shell, usually living in water, such as clams and snails.

nurse (v) — to feed young with milk from the mother.

organ — a group of cells and tissues with a specific purpose, such as an eye.

predators — animals that kill and eat other animals.

prey — animals that are killed and eaten by other animals.

remora — a type of fish that has a suction disk on its head so it can attach itself to other fishes.

reproduce — to create offspring.

retract — to draw back in.

ruse — a trick; a clever or deceitful action.

savanna — a flat landscape or plain, usually covered with grasses and scattered trees.

species — animals or plants closely related, often similar in behavior and appearance, that can breed together.

submissive — to be subject to another's authority.

tropical — belonging to the tropics, or the region centered on the equator and lying between the Tropic of Cancer (23.5° north of the equator) and the Tropic of Capricorn (23.5° south of the equator). This region is typically hot and humid.

BOOKS TO READ

Amazing World of Birds. Stephen Caitlin (Troll Communications)

Animal Families series. (Gareth Stevens)

Animal Magic series. (Gareth Stevens)

Animal Societies. Jeremy Cherfas (Lerner Group)

At Home in the Tide Pool. Alexander Wright (Charlesbridge Publishing)

Bees Dance and Whales Sing: The Mysteries of Animal Communications. Margery Facklam (Sierra)

Colors of the Sea series. Marie Bearanger and Eric Ethan (Gareth Stevens)

Dangerous Reptilian Creatures. Michel Peissel (Chelsea House)

ENDANGERED! series. Bob Burton (Gareth Stevens)

Extremely Weird Fishes. Sarah Lovett (John Muir)

In Peril series. Barbara J. Behm and Jean-Christophe Balouet (Gareth Stevens)

Life in a Pond. H. Mason (Durkin Hayes)

Secrets of the Animal World series. (Gareth Stevens)

Wonderful World of Animals series. (Gareth Stevens)

VIDEOS

Animal Life in a Tidepool. (AIMS Media)

Animal Reproduction. (AGC Educational Media)

Fish, Shellfish and Other Underwater Life. (Library Video)

How Animals Help Each Other. (Agency for Instructional Technology)

Mammal Mothers and Babies. (Phoenix/BFA Films & Video)

WEB SITES

www.neocomm.net/~eadams/cheetah.html

www.fws.gov/~r9extaff/biologues/ bio_elep.html

www.riverdale.k12.or.us/salmon.htm

www.ducks.org/puddler/frame_puzzles.html

INDEX